T0130403

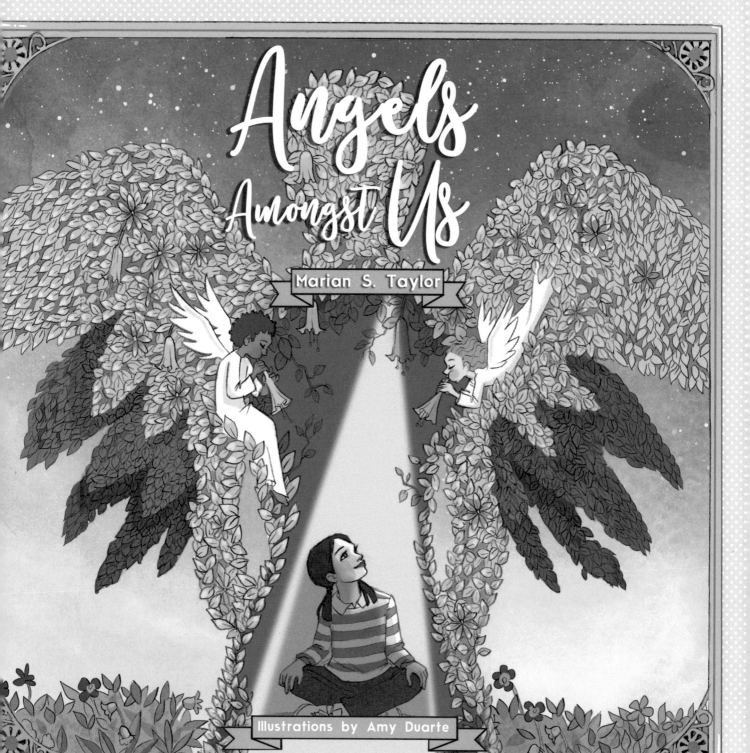

Angels
Amongst Us

Marian S. Taylor

Illustrations by Amy Duarte

Balboa Press books may be ordered through booksellers or by contacting:

Balboa Press
A Division of Hay House
1663 Liberty Drive
Bloomington, IN 47403
www.balboapress.com
844-682-1282

Because of the dynamic nature of the Internet, any web addresses or links contained in
this book may have changed since publication and may no longer be valid. The views
expressed in this work are solely those of the author and do not necessarily reflect the views
of the publisher, and the publisher hereby disclaims any responsibility for them.

ISBN: 978-1-9822-1710-5 (sc)
ISBN: 978-1-9822-1709-9 (e)

Library of Congress Control Number: 2018914526

Print information available on the last page.

Balboa Press rev. date: 08/26/2021

BALBOA.PRESS

Angels Amongst Us

As a little child I come to earth,
to be with loved ones dear.

I am excited to be here as I grow
and learn.
I am happy and without fear.

But there are times when I feel a little frightened.
Sometimes I feel alone and I feel bad.

And sometimes when I feel alone or frightened,
I also worry and feel very sad.

I have heard of guardian angels.
I have heard of the help God gives.

I have heard that angels are with me,
but I wonder where they live.

I want to feel them close beside me.
I want to see their loving face.

I want to know that God and His helpers
are with me.
I want to know that I am safe.

I know God can speak through parents,
friends, and helpers.
Whatever might be the choice.

It's important to trust my feelings inside.
I call it my heartfelt voice.

I want to know that God loves
and comforts me.
I want to know how this happens to be...

When God and His helper angels
are comforting me,
I want to understand the messages
and how to receive.

Sit back and listen to these words
God would say,

As He explains how His helper angels
send messages each day…

I may not look like you think I should look.
I may not sound like you think I should sound.

Listen for my voice in the words of a loved one,
Look for my face in the face of a friend.

Listen as I send you a message on the breeze.
Yes! I'm waving as I wiggle the leaves.

Sometimes I look like a shining light.
Sometimes I look like a cloud...

Sometimes I'm a thought in your mind that brings peace.
Sometimes I'm a familiar hug in a crowd…

*I can send you a message
through the words of other people.*

*I can send you a message
through the words of a song.*

I can give you a feeling of strength and hope...
No matter, you can't get this wrong.

*I and my helper angels are ready
and willing to assist,
Whenever you feel sad or frightened
or when you just need a lift.*

*Know that I AM with you and accept my love...
Love... sent on angels' wings...
Wings of light from above.*

Author: Marian S. Taylor

Marian S. Taylor, EdD, is a retired university professor. Her career began at the elementary level where she taught first grade and served as a reading specialist. She was director of the university laboratory school and a chairperson of a university department. She taught undergraduate and graduate classes while at the university and spent many years directing the program for the development of reading specialists.

Marian has been very involved with her family and with church activities. She is the mother of three grown children and is very proud of her grandchildren. Other publications can be viewed at

www.marianstaylor.com

Illustrator: Amy Duarte

Amy Duarte began her career as an artist working for Walt Disney Animation Studios. From there, she leapt into the world of visual effects and graphic arts on more than 30 feature films like "Pirates of the Caribbean: At World's End," "The Amazing Spiderman," "Mr. and Mrs. Smith," etc. She was appointed as a lead artist for several major motion pictures, including "Fantastic Four," where she advised and guided a team of artists on creating the special effects of Jessica Alba's character (Sue Storm).

Born in Jakarta, Indonesia, and raised in three different countries, Amy is fluent in six languages and an avid polo player. She was also on the design team that created the top secret commercial for Apple's Watch before the product was launched. Her portfolio can be viewed at www.amyduarte.com.

Printed in the United States
by Baker & Taylor Publisher Services